This book belongs to

____

Illustrated by Jack Button
Cover Design and Layout by Praise Saflor

ISBN 979-8-9879108-3-2 (Hardcover)
979-8-9879108-4-9 (Softcover)

JOY'S HOUSE

by Mahsan Boogert

Art by Jack Button

A little fairy is visiting me today.
I don't know where she came from.
    "Hi Joy!" the little fairy says.
"Why are you crying?"
    "I don't know. Maybe it's because I think
my grandma doesn't love me anymore.
My life seems so different now."

"How is it different?"
the fairy asks.

I tell the fairy all the things
my grandma used to do.
    She used to pick me up from
school every day.

I was always happy to see
her, and she always surprised
me with something special.

She used to take me to the library and
let me choose as many books as I wanted.
Then we read them together.

Grandma often said, "You're a good girl, Joy. Let's go to the ice cream shop." She even let me bring my best friend Lili along.

Grandma let us get as many scoops of ice cream as we wanted. I never could finish mine.

ICE CREAM
VANILLA
CHOCOLAT
STRAWBERRY
CREAM

Every Friday, my grandma and grandpa took me to the park. I played on the swing while Grandma pushed me. She laughed every time I screamed, "Higher, higher, higher!"

Higher!
Higher!
Higher!

Now everything is different. Grandma doesn't do any of those things anymore. When I ask her why she doesn't pick me up from school, she says she can't find her keys.

Most of the time, she doesn't even seem to remember my name.

And when I tell her I love her, she doesn't say she loves me too. She just nods her head.

The little fairy flutters onto my shoulder.
"Have you talked to your mom about this?"
she asks. "What did she say?"
I tell the fairy that my mom said my
grandma is sick. Mom also said the doctors
and scientists are working hard to make
medicine for people like my grandma. Mom
said some grandpas need the medicine too.
The doctors hope the new medicine will help
people to not forget things. I hope this is true.

"Little fairy," I ask, "do you have a magic wand to heal my grandma?"

"No," she says softly, "but I have a magic plant! So if you wipe your tears and put a beautiful smile on your face, I will tell you more about it. That's better."

The fairy says that if we put our thoughts together and make a wish, and then plant this flower, our wish will come true. I want to do that.

"Are you ready to plant this?" the fairy asks.

"YES, YES! I AM READY."

"There are a few more things that will help your grandma get better," the fairy says.

"Please tell me," I beg. "I will do anything to help my grandma. I love her so much!"

I LOVE
HER
SO MUCH!

The fairy is smiling as she asks me an unusual question.

"Okay, do you know how to make some healthy foods or drinks?"

This is exciting. "Yes!" I say. "I know how to make a yummy smoothie with veggies and fruits. I learned it from my best friend Lili."

"Perfect!" the fairy says with a great big smile.

The fairy also tells me that I need to take my grandma for walks, maybe several times a week. "Don't go too far," she says. "Grandma will get tired."

"Okay!"

"And do you have a family picture album?" she asks.

I tell her that we do have a big family album stuffed with lots and lots of pictures.

The fairy says, "Take it with you when you visit your grandma. As you show her each picture, be sure to say the name of the people in the picture."

"And one last thing," says the fairy.
"Play music for her and always be cheerful
when you are with her. Are you sure you
can do all of these things? It's a long list."

"Yes, little fairy," I say. "I can do it all."

The fairy tells me that it's time to go to bed. She tells me to think happy thoughts and imagine that all the fairies are with me to help my grandma.

"Good night, Joy."

"Good night, my little fairy!"

Before I know it, my mom is waking me up.
    "Joy, wake up! Today, we are going
to visit Grandma."
    "Oh wait, wait!" I say. "Look at my plant.
It is growing! I'd Like to give this to
Grandma today."

I see my grandpa when we walk in the door. I say Hi and give him a kiss.

"Where is Grandma?" I ask.

Grandpa's answer makes me smile.

"She is in the living room, looking at the photo album you gave her."

I run to my grandma.

"Hi Grandma. This is for you!" I say softly.

"I planted it by myself."

"Oh, it's beautiful. Thank you!" she says.

"I love you Nana!"

"I love you too, Joy!"

I LOVE YOU TOO, JOY!